PLANET EARTH

VOLCANOES

James Carson

The Bookwright Press
New York · 1984

PLANET EARTH

Coastlines
Volcanoes
The Oceans
Water on the Land
The Work of the Wind
Weather and Climate

First published in the United States in 1984 by
The Bookwright Press, 387 Park Avenue South,
New York, NY 10016

First published in 1983 by
Wayland (Publishers) Ltd
49 Lansdowne Place, Hove
East Sussex BN3 1HF, England

ISBN 0-531-04793-8

Library of Congress Catalog Card Number 83-72793

Printed in Italy by
G. Canale & C.S.p.A., Turin

Contents

OLIMN

The power of volcanoes

On February 5 AD 63, a very strong earthquake shook the area around what is now Naples, on Italy's west coast. Two of the towns in the region, Pompeii and Herculaneum, were badly shaken. But although they were built on the lower slopes of Mt. Vesuvius, the inhabitants did not think that the earthquake was linked with the volcano in any way—Vesuvius had been inactive for so long that they believed there was nothing to fear. They simply rebuilt the walls that had been knocked down, and went about their lives as usual.

Throughout the next 16 years, there were several more earthquakes, but the people of Pompeii and Herculaneum carried on, unaware of the danger they were in until the very last moment.

Then, on August 24 AD 79, Vesuvius burst into life and one of the most staggering eruptions in history began. In the morning, a large harmless-looking cloud appeared over the volcano. It grew rapidly, forming a vertical plume many thousands of meters high, and then flattening out. Vast quantities of volcanic ash began falling on Pompeii, completely blotting out the sun, and the volcano belched out choking fumes. As lightning flashed overhead and torrential rainstorms fell on the area, thousands of terrified people tried to escape in boats or on foot, but many remained in the town and were suffocated by the ash and fumes.

The eruption finally came to an end after two days, by which time Pompeii was buried under a carpet of ash over 3 meters (10 feet) deep. Most of the inhabitants were either dead or financially ruined. Herculaneum, on the other side of Vesuvius, was also buried, but in a different way. Great thicknesses of ash had piled up on the slopes above the town.

Opposite *When Vesuvius erupted in AD 79, the town of Pompeii was buried under a carpet of ash, and many of the inhabitants were suffocated.*

The heavy rainfall mixed with this ash to form something like a thick layer of liquid cement. Eventually, this began to slide down in the form of giant mudflows which gathered speed and picked up more material as they went. Some of these mudflows rushed through the town of Herculaneum, smothering parts of it in a mass of mud and boulders 20 meters (65 feet) deep.

Both towns lay hidden and forgotten for almost 1,700 years. When they were first rediscovered, pits were dug in a haphazard way and statues, coins and jewelery were plundered. Later, archaeologists began digging more methodically, and much of Pompeii has been excavated. It is now possible to stroll through the streets of the town, looking at the remains

The streets of Pompeii as they are today.

of shops, houses and villas on either side. During the digging, the outlines of many bodies were found buried in the hardened ash, and archaeologists were able to pour plaster of Paris into the hollow "molds" to make casts. Excavation work has also been carried out at Herculaneum. It is more difficult there because the mud has set much harder than the ash that covered Pompeii, and because a new town has been built on top of the site of the old one.

As we shall see, not all volcanic eruptions are like the one that buried Pompeii and Herculaneum—in fact, no two eruptions are exactly the same. Some are very gentle, whereas others are enormously violent. In many ways they are highly destructive, but they also have their uses. Let us now look more closely at what happens when volcanoes erupt.

The body cast of a victim of the Vesuvius eruption.

Volcanic eruptions

What comes out of a volcano?

The material that rises up inside an erupting volcano is called **magma.** It is a mixture of molten rock and gas—two of the main products of an eruption.

When magma rises inside a volcano,

When Vesuvius erupted in 1906, its height was reduced by 110 meters (360 feet); this is what it looks like today.

the gas tries to escape from the molten rock. If the molten rock is very runny, the gas can escape easily and the volcano erupts gently. But if it is thick, the gas cannot escape so easily and it explodes before it reaches the surface—this often produces very violent eruptions.

Gas can sometimes play the major part in an eruption. For example, when Vesuvius erupted again in 1906, gas was blasted with enormous force to a height of 13 kilometers (8 miles). This eruption, which lasted 18 hours, reduced the height of the mountain by 110 meters (360 feet).

Besides gas, most volcanoes also pour out some molten rock. When it flows out of the volcano, molten rock is called **lava**. It is very hot—usually between 900 and 1,200°C (1,650-2,200°F)—but it eventually cools to become solid rock again. As we know, molten rock inside a volcano may be thick or runny, and this also applies to the lava when it comes out of a volcano. Thick lava does not flow very far during an eruption, and it tends to pile up close to the mouth or vent of the volcano. It may even solidify inside the volcano, and if this happens, a large explosion is needed to unblock the vent.

A fountain of runny lava, 350 meters (1,150 feet) high, is thrown out of Kilauea, Hawaii.

Runny lavas can flow for long distances before they become solid, even if the ground does not slope very much. Some lava flows in the Columbia River plateau in the northwestern United States are 200 kilometers (125 miles) long, and cover an area that is almost horizontal.

A volcano may produce runny lava during one eruption, and thick lava during the next. The type of lava seems to depend on the length of time between eruptions—after a long gap, the lava is usually thick and the activity is more violent.

During an explosive eruption, fragments of rock, known as **pyroclasts**, are blown out. The size of these fragments varies greatly and they are given different names according to their size. **Ash** consists of particles that are less than 4 millimeters (0.16 in.) across, while fragments between 4 and 32 millimeters

A solidified volcanic bomb.

(0.16-1.25 in.) are called **lapilli** (the Italian word for "little stones"). Larger lumps are called **blocks** if they are solid, or **bombs** if they are molten.

All of these fragments build up around the volcano. The smaller particles travel farther because they are blown by the wind. Very small ash particles can also be thrown high up into the atmosphere; after the eruption of Mt. St. Helens, in the state of Washington, in May 1980, scientists were worried that the huge quantity of ash

The eruption of Mt. St. Helens, in the state of Washington, in 1980, produced massive quantities of volcanic ash.

that was blown out would affect the Earth's climate for many years to come.

When ash is blown high into the atmosphere, it can sometimes cause torrential rainstorms. When the rain reaches the ground, it mixes with the material that has fallen around the volcano and triggers off huge **mudflows** that sweep down at speeds of up to 90 kilometers per hour (60 miles per hour). Mudflows like this are common in Indonesia, particularly on Kelut volcano, Java.

One of the rarest and most dangerous results of an eruption is called a **glowing cloud**. This is a cloud of very hot volcanic ash and gas that spills out of a volcano and rushes silently downhill at up to 200 kilometers per hour (125 miles per hour). In 1902, Mt. Pelée in the West Indies erupted in a huge explosion that sent a glowing cloud sweeping down into the town of St Pierre. It moved so fast that massive stone walls were blown down, and the heat of the cloud killed almost everyone in its path: of the 30,000 people in the town, only two survived.

Opposite *As a plume of ash rises from Mt. Mayon, in the Philippines, a "glowing cloud" rushes down the mountainside.*

Types of eruptions

Despite their differences, eruptions can be divided into several groups, which are named after outstanding examples.

Hawaiian eruptions are the quietest of all. Their lava is very runny and the gas can escape easily without explosions. Sometimes, however, fountains of liquid rock are thrown high into the air. If the spray is caught by the wind, it is drawn out

A smouldering "fire pit" in the crater of Mauna Loa, Hawaii.

into long, glassy threads, called "Pele's hair" (after Pele, the Hawaiian goddess of volcanoes). Kilauea, in Hawaii, is a good example of this type.

Strombolian eruptions are slightly more violent. They are named after Stromboli, a tiny volcanic island off Italy, which has been erupting frequently for hundreds of years. The lava is not quite as runny as in a Hawaiian eruption, and every few minutes there is an explosion that hurls bombs into the air. These explosions are usually too small to be dangerous—there are two villages quite close to the mouth of Stromboli, and their inhabitants know that they have little to fear from the volcano.

The next type of eruption is called *Vulcanian*, after another Italian island, Vulcano. This kind of eruption is much more violent than a Strombolian one. The lava tends to be quite thick, and the series of explosions caused by the escaping gas can often blow away parts of the volcano itself. Large quantities of solid blocks and ash are thrown into the air, and a huge

Opposite *Stromboli, erupting at night.*

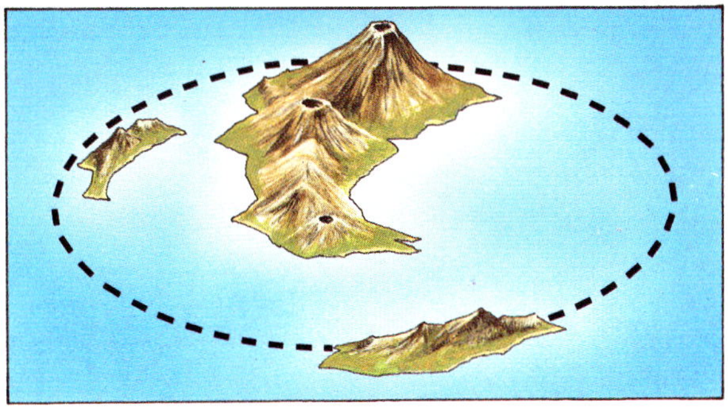

Krakatoa before 1883 . . .

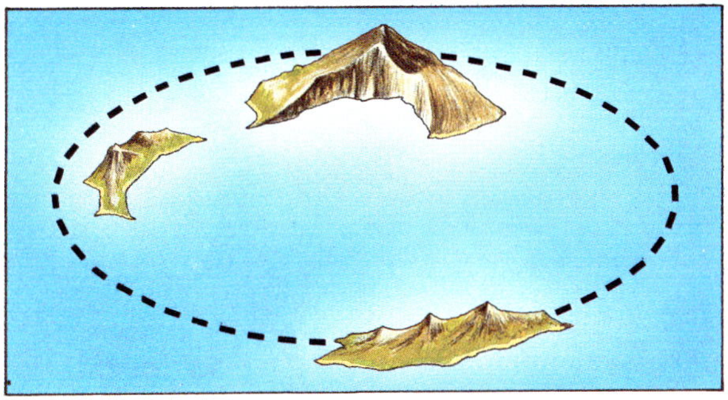

. . . immediately afterward . . .

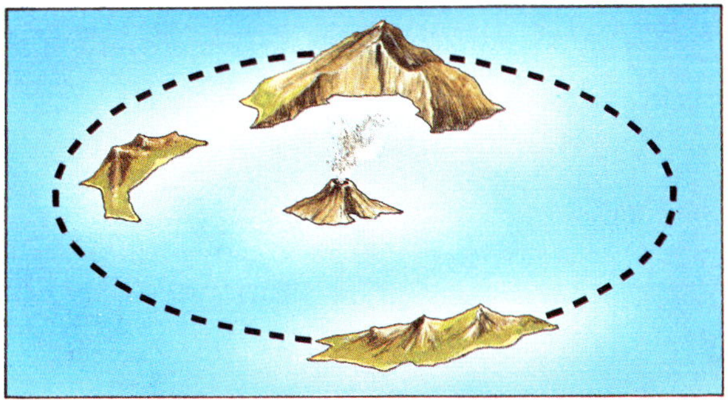

. . . and Anak Krakatoa, which appeared during the 1920s.

plume of gas and fine ash rises above the crater, often to a height of several kilometers.

A *Vesuvian* eruption is similar to a Vulcanian, but there tends to be a continuous explosive blast that may last for several hours. Even more pyroclasts are blown out, and clouds of ash are carried very high into the air.

Plinian eruptions also take their name, indirectly, from Vesuvius—Pliny the Younger was a Roman who wrote about the disastrous eruption of Vesuvius in AD 79. Even more pyroclasts are ejected than in a Vesuvian eruption, often with such force that large parts of the volcano are destroyed or collapse. In 1883, the island of Krakatoa, between Sumatra and Java, suffered just such a fate. The explosions were heard more than 4,800 kilometers (3,000 miles) away and the collapse of the island produced huge waves (or **tsunamis**) up to 35 meters (115 feet) high. These tsunamis rushed onto the shores of Sumatra and Java, devastating 300 towns and villages and killing 36,000 people.

One of the main features of a *Peléean* eruption is the formation of glowing clouds (see page 13). The lava is very thick, and it often builds up into a plug, blocking the mouth or vent of the volcano. This plug can only be removed by violent gas explosions, which throw out glowing clouds.

A large number of the world's volcanoes lie beneath the sea, and their eruptions sometimes create new land. At first, ash is blown up out of the sea and high into the air, and a white column of steam rises up. Then a pile of ejected material builds up on the sea floor until the top of it appears above sea-level. When the volcano is well above sea-level, lava begins to flow and small explosions occur, as in a Strombolian eruption. This is how the **volcanic island** of Surtsey was created off Iceland in 1963.

Opposite *Lava pours into the sea from the new island of Surtsey, Iceland.*

Volcanic shapes

Volcanic mountains are made up of ash, lava and rocks. After a few eruptions, a small hill begins to form around the vent. The hill grows as more and more layers are deposited by successive eruptions, and it may eventually become hundreds or even thousands of meters high.

When most people think of a volcano, they imagine a graceful, cone-shaped mountain with a crater at the top. But, as you can see from the pictures in this book, not all volcanoes are like that. The shape of a volcano depends largely on what comes out of it during its eruptions.

Strato-volcanoes are composed of alternate layers of ash and lava.

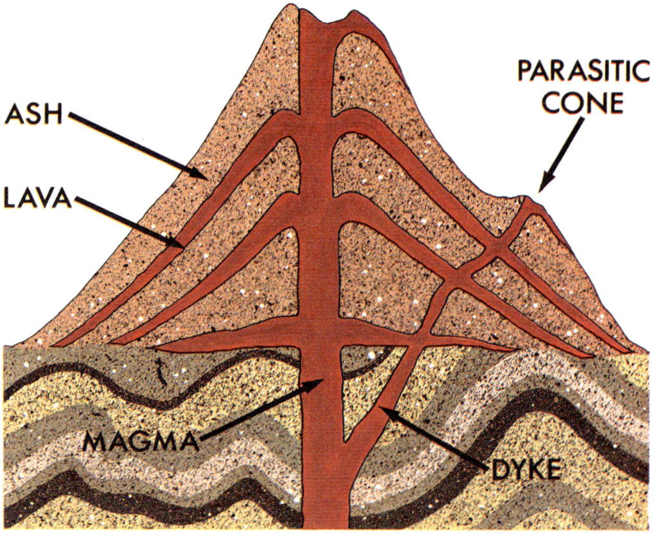

Cones, craters and calderas

When thick lava is erupted, it comes out almost like toothpaste from a tube. It flows very slowly, and usually solidifies before it travels very far. For this reason, thick lava builds up into rough, steep-sided cones.

The elegant, cone-shaped mountains mentioned above are called **strato-volcanoes**. They develop from different kinds of eruptions. Some, like the famous Mt. Fuji in Japan, are the result of many short flows of runny lava piled one on top of another. More usually, strato-volcanoes are built up of layers of pyroclasts that become thinner the farther

Opposite *The graceful, snow-capped cone of Mt. Fuji, Japan.*

away they are from the vent. In between these layers there are solidified lava flows. Because of this, strato-volcanoes are also called composite volcanoes.

Where eruptions produce mainly pyroclasts, the result is often an **ash** or **cinder cone**. This is simply a pile of loose material around the vent of the volcano.

The funnel-shaped hollow at the top of a volcanic cone is called the **crater**. The bottom of the funnel opens into the pipe through which the magma finds its way to the surface. Craters are usually fairly small—less than a kilometer (3,300 feet) in diameter and up to 150 meters (500 feet) deep. Some, however, are much larger: Mt. Antakihak in Alaska, for example, has a crater that is nearly 9 kilometers (5.5 miles) in diameter.

The largest volcanic craters are sometimes called **calderas**. They are formed either when a crater collapses in on itself because it is no longer supported underneath, or when a crater is enlarged by a very violent explosion. The world's largest caldera, at Mt. Aso in Japan, measures 27 by 16 kilometers (17 by 10 miles). The largest known volcano is Olympus Mons on the planet Mars; it is a staggering 600 kilometers (375 miles) in diameter and its caldera is 80 kilometers (50 miles) across.

Besides the crater at the top, many volcanoes develop additional vents on their sides. Etna, for example, has more than 200. Volcanic material often builds up around these vents, and the cones that develop are called **parasitic cones**.

Shield volcanoes and lava plateaus

Shield volcanoes are shaped rather like large, upturned saucers. They are formed by frequent eruptions of very runny lava, which spreads out over a great area around the vent before it becomes solid. There are several very good examples of shield volcanoes in the Hawaiian Islands, especially Mauna Loa, the largest volcano on Earth. At its base on the sea floor, it measures about 120 kilometers (75 miles) across, and is over 9 kilometers (5.5 miles) high.

Many millions of years ago, huge

Opposite *The world's largest caldera, at Mt. Aso in Japan.*

amounts of runny lava were erupted from long fissures or cracks in the Earth's surface. The lava spread out over vast areas and built up to form thick plateaus, completely covering the original hills and valleys. The Deccan in India is a lava plateau. It now covers about 250,000 square kilometers (96,500 square miles), but it may originally have been twice this size. Two of Britain's most famous landmarks—the Giant's Causeway in Antrim, Northern Ireland, and Fingal's Cave on the Scottish island of Staffa—were developed during the formation of a huge lava plateau about 60 million years ago. They are made up of thousands of columns, mostly six-sided, which formed when the thick lava cooled and shrank.

Above *Mauna Kea, a Hawaiian shield volcano. Compare its shape with that of Mt. Fuji shown on page 19.*

Opposite *The Giant's Causeway in Antrim, Northern Ireland.*

Plugs, dikes, and sills

When a volcano ceases to be active, the old vent often remains filled up with solidified lava, which is harder and more resistant to erosion than the rest of the mountain. Over several thousand years, most of the mountain is worn away, leaving the tough lava in the form of a pinnacle of rock, called a **plug**. Millions of years ago, there were volcanoes in various parts of Britain; and in Edinburgh, Scotland, there are five volcanic plugs, including the hill known as Castle Rock.

The most spectacular example of a plug is Ship Rock in the New Mexico desert. It rises vertically from the flat desert floor,

Ship Rock, in the New Mexico desert, is a dramatic example of a volcanic plug.

reaching 430 meters (1,400 feet) at its highest point.

Sometimes magma forces its way into cracks and joints in the rocks underground, and cools down and solidifies below the surface. Like volcanic plugs, these "intrusions" of **igneous rock** (solidified magma) are only seen at the surface if the overlying rocks have been eroded away. **Dikes** are formed in this way when magma rises through near-vertical fissures and cools to form solid "walls" of rock. Two remarkable dikes run west and south from Ship Rock, rising 60 to 90 meters (195-295 feet) above the desert. Dikes sometimes occur in large "swarms"; there are hundreds of parallel dikes in northwest Scotland, particularly on the islands of Mull and Arran.

A swarm of volcanic dikes have been exposed by the erosion of this cliff-face.

Sills are sheets of igneous rock similar to dikes except that they lie roughly horizontally between layers of other rock. They can be of almost any thickness, and may extend over very large areas. The most striking example in Britain is the Great Whin Sill. It varies in thickness from 1 to 70 meters (3-230 feet), and covers over 4,000 square kilometers (1,500 square miles), from the Farne Islands and the Northumbrian coast, across England to the western edge of the Pennine hills.

Hadrian's Wall running along the crest of the Great Whin Sill in Northumberland, England.

Underneath a volcano

Where magma comes from

Our planet is made up of three layers. The part we live on, the thin outer skin, is called the **crust**. On average it is about 30 kilometers (18 miles) thick, although beneath high mountain ranges it may be more than 50 kilometers (30 miles). Under the oceans, the crust is much thinner—about 8-10 kilometers (5-6 miles).

The three layers that make up our planet.

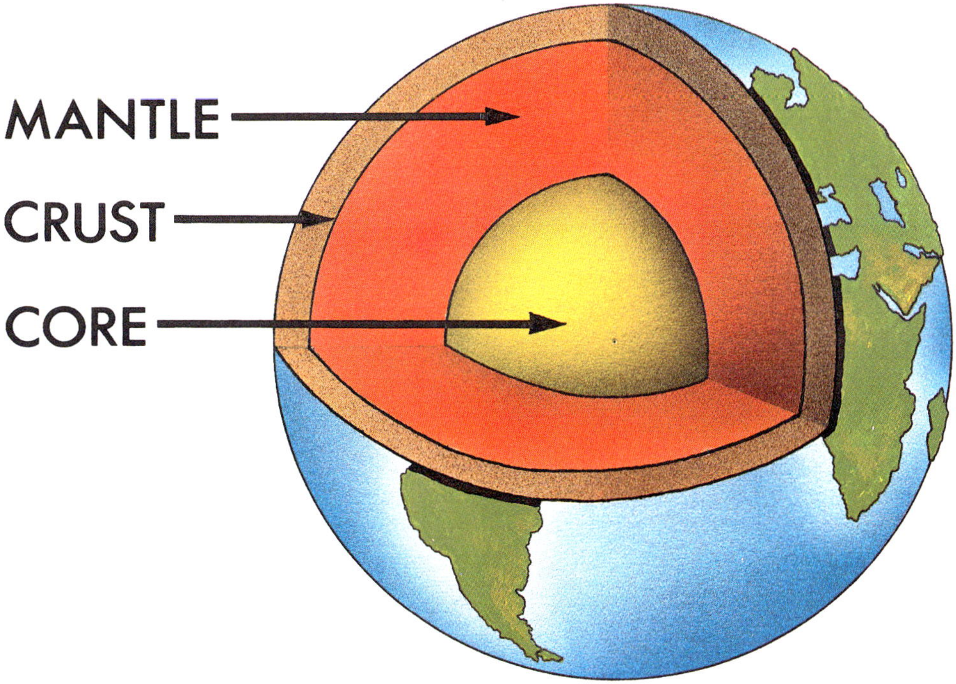

The layer below the crust is the **mantle**. It is much thicker, extending to a depth of about 2,900 kilometers (1,800 miles). The innermost part of the Earth is the **core**.

As we travel down through the layers, the temperature rises—at the center of the Earth the temperature is thought to be about 4,000°C (7,200°F). Despite this, most of the Earth is solid because the pressure also increases with depth.

Magma, the material that "feeds" volcanoes, comes from the lower part of the crust and the upper part of the mantle. At this level it is hot enough, and the pressure is just low enough, for a small amount of the rock to melt, producing the magma. Besides molten rock, the magma also contains many bubbles of gas.

Why volcanoes erupt

If enough magma is formed, it begins to rise up toward the surface through cracks in the Earth's crust. As this happens, the bubbles of gas grow larger and try to escape from the molten rock. Finally

Magma rising up through the Earth's crust and appearing at the surface during a volcanic eruption.

when the bubbles are so large that they cannot be held back, the volcano erupts, pouring out gas, lava and pyroclasts.

Active, dormant and extinct volcanoes

Volcanoes usually pass through three stages in their life cycle. At first, eruptions are frequent, and the volcano is said to be **active**. If a long time has passed since the last eruption but it is thought that it may erupt again in the future, the volcano is called **dormant** (sleeping). An **extinct** (or dead) volcano is one that has shown no signs of activity for so long that scientists think it will never erupt again.

It is sometimes difficult to say whether volcanoes are dormant or extinct, for they can lie dormant for decades or for thousands of years. The 1973 eruption on Heimaey, Iceland, came as a complete surprise since Helgafell, the largest volcano on the island, had been dormant for about 5,000 years.

Alternatively, people may not have records that date back as far as the last eruption; until AD 79, the Romans thought that Vesuvius was extinct, since there was no record of eruptions.

The 1973 eruption on the island of Heimaey, Iceland.

The world's volcanoes

At present, there are about 530 known active volcanoes in the world and many thousands of extinct ones.

Although every continent except Australia has some volcanoes, they are positioned in a very strange way. In North America, for example, there are volcanoes only down the western side,

Most volcanoes (in red) lie close to the boundaries between the "plates" that make up the Earth's crust. The thick, black lines show where one plate is diving down beneath another, and the thinner lines show where new crust is being created.

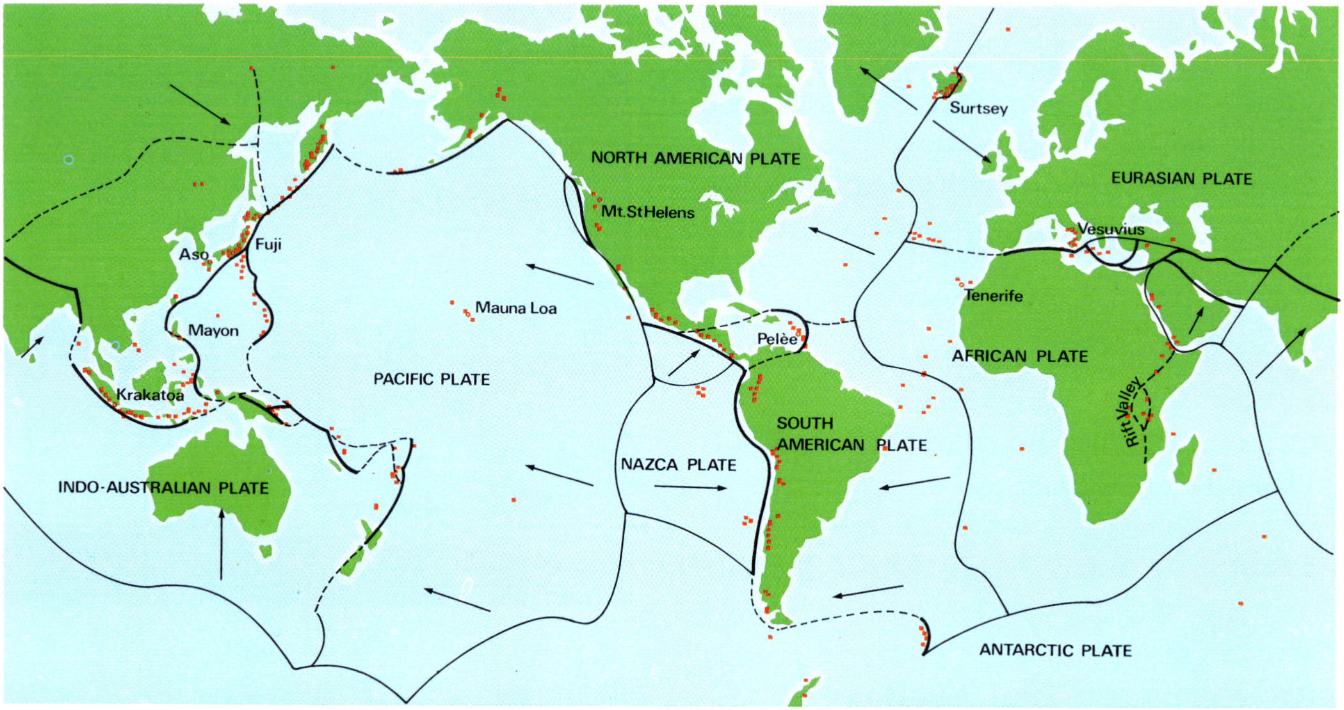

and most European volcanoes occur in the region of the central Mediterranean.

There are about 80 active volcanoes under the oceans. At first they erupt underwater, but they may eventually build up to form volcanic islands. Tristan da Cunha, the Hawaiian islands, and Surtsey were all formed in this way.

The drifting continents

As we have seen, volcanoes appear above cracks in the Earth's crust. If you look at the map on the facing page, you will see most of the world's volcanoes marked. The black lines show large cracks in the crust, and most volcanoes lie very close to these cracks.

The cracks are really the boundaries between huge **plates** that make up the crust, fitting together like pieces in a jigsaw puzzle. However, unlike a jigsaw, the plates are actually moving.

About 200 million years ago the surface of the Earth looked very different. There was just one enormous supercontinent, called Pangaea. This comprised two parts—Laurasia, consisting of Europe, North America and Asia; and Gondwanaland, consisting of Africa,

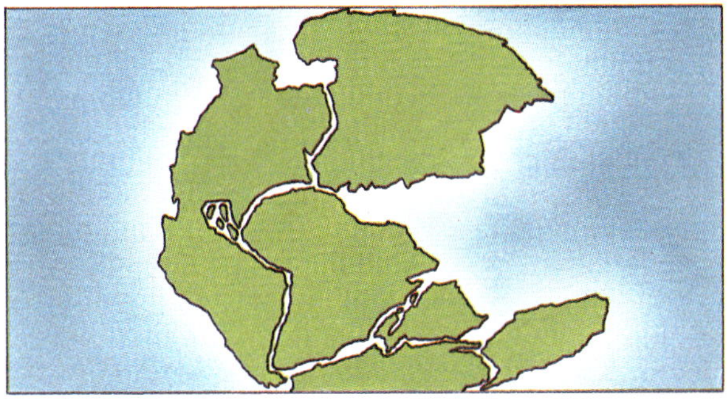

The Earth 200 million years ago . . .

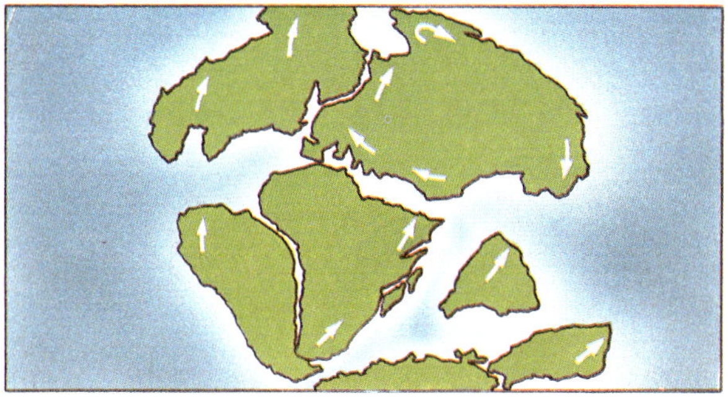

. . . and 135 million years ago.

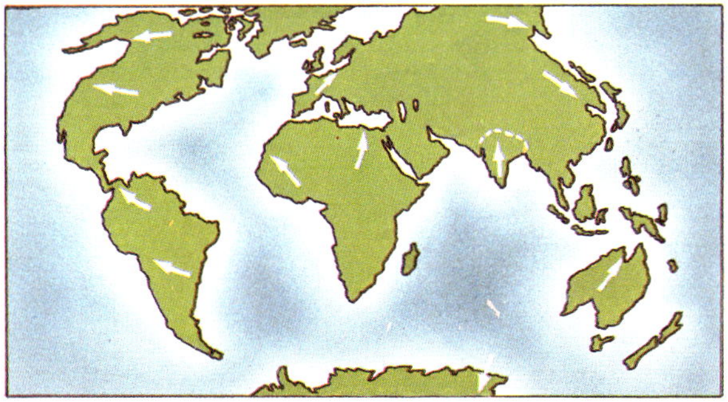

This is how the Earth looks today, but the continents are still moving.

South America and Australia.

Then this supercontinent began to break up; the plates literally drifted apart, and they are still moving today. In some places, the giant plates are pushing against each other—along the west coast of South America, for example. Here, the thin oceanic crust of the Nazca Plate collides with the thicker South American Plate. Instead of piling up in a great heap, the Nazca Plate dives down under the South American Plate. Although the plates are moving very slowly, enormous forces are involved, and as one pushes down past another, there is a great deal of friction. This friction produces earthquakes and heat — if you rub your hands together, you will notice that they become warm—and the heat causes the rocks to melt. Some of this molten rock, or magma, finds its way up to the surface, causing the chain of volcanoes running

Opposite *This is what the Atlantic Ocean would look like if the water were drained out. Note the ridge running down the center, where new crust is made.*

Below *Along the west coast of South America one plate dives down below another, and the friction causes rocks to melt and rise to the surface.*

Azores
Canary Is.
Cape Verde Is.
MID-ATLANTIC RIDGE
St Helena

down the western edge of South America. But much of the magma solidifies before it reaches the surface, to form vast masses of igneous rock called **batholiths**.

In other places, two plates seem to be moving away from each other—down the middle of the Atlantic Ocean, for example. Here, new oceanic crust is actually being made. As the two plates move apart, magma rises up to fill the gap between them. This produces a high ridge, often with undersea volcanoes. Some of these volcanoes build up to form islands.

Some volcanoes occur a great distance from the boundaries between the plates. Those that form the Hawaiian islands are almost in the center of the Pacific Plate. They are the result of so-called "hot spots"—places where the temperature below the surface is higher than usual. At these hot spots a large amount of magma is produced, and it rises up through the crust and appears as shield volcanoes.

The volcanoes of East Africa occur for a different reason. They are found along the line of the East African rift system—

Kilimanjaro, in Kenya—one of the volcanoes of the rift system in East Africa.

A volcanic observatory, Maui, Hawaii.

a series of narrow, steep-sided valleys produced when the crust cracked, allowing blocks of land to drop downward. The cracking also made it possible for magma to rise up to the surface.

Can eruptions be predicted?

If scientists knew when a volcano was about to erupt, they could make sure that everyone was moved out of the danger zone, and many lives could be saved.

The main problem is the fact that all volcanoes behave in different ways, and this means that there is no clear set of signs that can be used to predict eruptions throughout the world.

The answer is to observe each individual volcano and learn to recognize the warnings it gives before it erupts. With this in mind, observatories have been built on many volcanoes in recent years.

Before an eruption, large amounts of magma begin to move deep below the volcano, and this triggers small earthquakes. Volcanic observatories have instruments, called **seismometers**, that can detect these earthquakes. Then, just prior to eruption, scientists can find out exactly from where the volcano will erupt, by using small, portable seismometers.

A small, portable seismometer.

Some eruptions in the Hawaiian islands are preceded by a strange, low humming or roaring noise. The local people call this "hearing Pele" (the Hawaiian goddess of volcanoes), but no one really knows what causes the noise. Nonetheless, it does help to warn people that they may be in danger.

Many volcanoes swell up a little before they erupt, and this swelling can be detected by using a **tiltmeter**. This consists of two bowls of liquid that are spaced far apart and connected by a tube. The levels of liquid in each bowl are carefully measured and recorded. When the volcano swells, one bowl is lifted up and the liquid runs downhill, raising the level in the lower bowl. Although this method sounds rather simple, modern tiltmeters are extremely sensitive. If a number of them are spaced out around a volcano, scientists can keep a very close watch on what is happening.

Uses of volcanoes

As you know, volcanoes can be highly destructive—they can cause great loss of life and damage to property, agricultural land, roads, and so on. But, strangely enough, they also have many uses.

Farming

Some lava flows of long ago have been broken down over the centuries to produce very fertile soils. This has occurred in Java, Indonesia; on the north-west part of the Deccan plateau, India; and on the plains around Etna, Sicily.

Soil derived from volcanic ash is also

Terrace farming on the poor soil of Tenerife, one of the Canary Islands.

fertile. In tropical areas, where nutrients are washed out of the topsoil by the heavy rains, a light ash fall is a welcome fertilizer.

In parts of the volcanic Canary Islands of Tenerife and Lanzarote, where there is little soil and low rainfall, a system of farming known as *enarenado* has been developed. The farmers have created fields on the rugged expanses of lava by spreading first a layer of soil and then volcanic ash. The ash soaks up water from dew, and this makes up for the poor rainfall. In this way, good crops of onions, tomatoes and potatoes can be grown on what was originally a desert of lava.

Yellow crystals of sulfur—one of the minerals formed by volcanic activity.

Minerals and gems

Volcanic activity sometimes results in the formation of minerals and precious stones. Before the twentieth century, there was a long period when almost all of the world's gold and silver was mined from volcanic rocks in North and South America. Larger sources of these metals have since been found elsewhere.

Large amounts of copper have also originated from volcanic activity, notably in Butte, Montana, and El Teniente, Chile. Other useful mineral deposits include bauxite, nickel, borax and sulfur.

Hot water

The power that causes volcanoes to erupt is not always violent. In New Zealand, for example, the hot magma and gas that lie deep underground do not often bring about eruptions. Instead, the gas seeps through the Earth's crust and, when it is near to the surface, it heats up water in the ground. This can produce geysers, hot springs, and pools of bubbling mud.

A **geyser** shoots a jet of boiling water and steam high into the air—the record height is 457 meters (1,500 feet). One of the most famous geysers is "Old Faithful" in the Yellowstone National Park, in Wyoming, which gushes about once every hour. There are others in Iceland, New Zealand, Japan and elsewhere.

Sometimes the hot water and steam escape much more gently, producing **hot springs** that bubble and hiss continuously, or hot, bubbling **mudpools**.

Scientists are learning how to put this hot water and steam to good use. In Iceland, for example, natural hot water is used to heat homes, greenhouses and swimming pools. More important, the steam can be used to drive turbines to generate electricity. There are so-called **geothermal** power stations at Larderello in Italy; Wairakei, New Zealand; The Geysers, California; and Krafla, Iceland.

In the future it may even be possible to produce geothermal energy in volcanic areas where there are no geysers or hot springs. Some scientists believe that water could be pumped down into the hot, dry rock above a mass of magma. The water would turn to steam, and this would then rise up to the surface through a pipe to drive a power station turbine and generate electricity.

Above *The geothermal power station at Krafla, Iceland. Steam escaping from the Earth is used to produce electricity.*

Opposite *Old Faithful geyser, in Yellowstone National Park.*

Scenic effects

In addition to their other uses, volcanoes are often exciting tourist attractions. Many vacationers visit Vesuvius, the volcano near Naples, Italy. They can climb to the top and look down into the crater, and visit the ruins of Pompeii and Herculaneum, the towns that were buried when Vesuvius erupted in AD 79.

Two other Italian volcanoes, Etna and Stromboli, are also popular sights. Boatloads of tourists are taken to see the small volcanic island of Stromboli, which erupts almost continuously; and vacationers can ski on the snowy slopes of Etna.

Tourists visiting the crater of Vesuvius, near Naples, Italy.

One of the most fascinating beauty spots in the U.S. is Crater Lake, Oregon. The lake is inside the huge caldera of an extinct volcano. This caldera, which is 10 kilometers (6 miles) across, was produced by an enormous eruption about 6,000 years ago.

There are, of course, many other interesting volcanoes and volcanic landforms throughout the world—the near-symmetrical, snow-capped cone of Mt. Fuji in Japan, and the Giant's Causeway in Northern Ireland, for example. If you ever get the chance to visit one, don't miss it!

Opposite *One of the most famous beauty spots in the U.S.—Crater Lake, in Oregon. It has formed in the caldera of an extinct volcano, and Wizard Island, in the center, is another extinct volcano.*

Facts and figures

The highest active volcano in the world is Antofalla in Argentina, at 6,450 meters (21,162 feet).

The highest extinct volcano is Cerro Aconcagua in Argentina, at 6,960 meters (22,834 feet).

The largest volcano is Mauna Loa in the Hawaiian Islands; at its base it measures 119 kilometers (74 miles) across.

The largest caldera is that of Mt. Aso in Japan, which measures 27 by 16 kilometers (17 by 10 miles).

The greatest volume of matter discharged during a volcanic eruption was in the 1815 eruption of Tambora, Indonesia; it has been estimated at more than 150 cubic kilometers (36 cubic miles). As a result, the height of the mountain was reduced by about 1,250 meters (4,100 feet).

The greatest volcanic explosion occurred when the island of Santorini in the Aegean Sea blew up in about 1470 BC. The greatest recorded explosion was that of Krakatoa, in the Sunda Strait between Java and Sumatra, on August 27, 1883. The sound was heard more than 4,800 kilometers (3,000 miles) away.

The longest lava flow in historic times is from the 1783 eruption of Laki in southeast Iceland, which flowed 65-70 kilometers (40.5-43.5 miles). The longest known lava flow is the Roza flow in North America, with a length of 480 kilometers (300 miles); it was produced about 15 million years ago.

The tallest geyser in the world is Waimangu in New Zealand, which erupted to a height of more than 457 meters (1,500 feet) in 1904. However, it has not been active since 1917.

Glossary

Active The term for a volcano that erupts frequently.

Ash The smallest pyroclastic particles—less than 4mm (0.16 in.) across.

Ash cone or **cinder cone** A pile of loose pyroclastic material that builds up around a volcanic vent.

Batholith A large mass of magma that solidifies underground.

Blocks and **bombs** Pyroclasts that are larger than 32mm (1.25 in.) across; blocks are solid lumps, and bombs are molten.

Caldera A large, basin-shaped crater bounded by steep cliffs, often formed by the collapse of the top of a volcanic mountain, and sometimes occupied by a lake.

Core The innermost layer of the Earth.

Crater The funnel-shaped hollow at the top of a volcano.

Crater lake A lake that forms in the crater of an extinct volcano.

Crust The surface "skin" of the Earth—the part we live on.

Dormant The term for a volcano that has not erupted for a long time but is likely to erupt again in the future.

Dike A vertical or near-vertical sheet of igneous rock, formed when magma forces its way upward through the rocks near the Earth's surface and then cools and solidifies.

Earthquake A movement or tremor of the Earth's crust (the outer layer of rock). Earthquakes can be caused by volcanic explosions, and they often precede or accompany eruptions.

Eruption The forcing of volcanic material (solid, liquid and gaseous) from the interior of the Earth through a vent at the surface.

Extinct The term for a volcano that has not erupted for so long that scientists think it will never erupt again.

Geothermal power Power that is made using the heat of the Earth's interior.

Geyser A spring that throws a jet of hot water and steam into the air at regular or irregular intervals. Geysers only occur in volcanic regions.

Glowing cloud A cloud of very hot volcanic ash and gas that rolls down the side of a volcano, destroying everything in its path.

Hot spring A spring caused by hot water and steam escaping gently from below the Earth's surface.

Igneous rock Rock that has solidified from molten magma. It may have cooled and solidified below the surface or after having been ejected from a volcano in the form of lava. There are many different kinds of igneous rock.

Lapilli The name for pyroclasts that are between 4 and 32mm (0.16 and 1.25 inches) across.

Lava Molten rock or magma that has been forced to the surface in a volcanic eruption.

Magma The molten rock that forms below the solid rock of the Earth's crust and sometimes reaches the surface as lava.

Mantle The layer of the Earth that is between the crust and the core.

Mudflow A mixture of pyroclasts and rainwater, which flows down the side of a volcano at high speed.

Mudpool A pool of bubbling mud caused by the gentle escape of hot water and steam from below the Earth's surface.

Parasitic cone A cone formed when volcanic material is erupted from a vent on the side of a volcanic mountain.

Plates The rigid pieces of which the Earth's crust is composed.

Plug A column of lava that solidifies in the central pipe of a volcano and later becomes exposed when the rest of the mountain is eroded away.

Pyroclasts The name for the solid material ejected from a volcano; it includes ash, lapilli, blocks and bombs.

Seismometer An instrument for detecting earthquakes.

Sill A horizontal or near-horizontal sheet of igneous rock, formed when magma forced its way between two layers of other rock, and then solidified.

Strato-volcano A volcano composed of alternating layers of pyroclasts and lava.

Tiltmeter An instrument that can detect the slight swelling of a volcano before an eruption.

Volcanic island An island created by the eruptions of an underwater volcano.

Further reading

Aylesworth, Thomas G. *Geological Disasters: Earthquakes and Volcanoes.* New York: Franklin Watts, 1979.

Berger, Melvin. *Disastrous Volcanoes.* New York: Franklin Watts, 1981

Fodor, Ronald V. *Earth Afire! Volcanoes and Their Activities.* New York: William Morrow, 1981.

Fradin, Dennis. *Volcanoes.* Chicago: Childrens Press, 1982.

Harris, Susan. *Volcanoes.* New York: Franklin Watts, 1979

Place, Marian T. *Mount St. Helens: A Sleeping Volcano Awakes.* New York: Dodd, Mead, 1980.

Poynter, Margaret. *Volcanoes: The Fiery Mountains.* New York: Julian Messner, 1980.

Radlauer, Ed. *Volcano Mania.* Chicago: Childrens Press, 1981.

Index

Picture acknowledgements

The illustrations in this book were supplied by: Melinda Berge 6, 7, Gerald Cubitt 34, Nicholas Devore 35, Wedigo Ferchland 29, Leonard Lee Rue 40, Werner Stoy 22—all from Bruce Coleman; Bill Donohoe 15, 18, 27, 28, 31, 32; Geoscience Features 12, 14, 24, 25, 26, 36, 37; Italian National Tourist Office 8, 42; Japan Information Centre 19; Japan National Tourist Organization 21; Anna Jupp 33; Northern Ireland Tourist Board 23; Photo Research International 13, 38, 43; Solarfilma 17; Malcolm S. Walker 4, 30; David R. Williams 10, 41; Zefa *front cover*, 9, 11.